Heidi & Daniel Howarth

What Makes Me Happy?

Sky Pony Press
New York

Little Panda stretched and she yawned, but she wasn't ready
to get up yet.
Cuddled up close in her mommy's soft fur, she was as comfortable
as a baby panda could be.

The bright sun warmed her fur.
"Come on," whispered Mommy, "let's go
and find some yummy shoots."

They left their warm, safe cave. Little Panda stopped for a second. From high on the hill by the cave she could see the whole valley. The tall, green bamboo swayed gently in the soft breeze.

She loved her warm, snuggly cave, but her empty tummy was grumbling. It was time to eat.

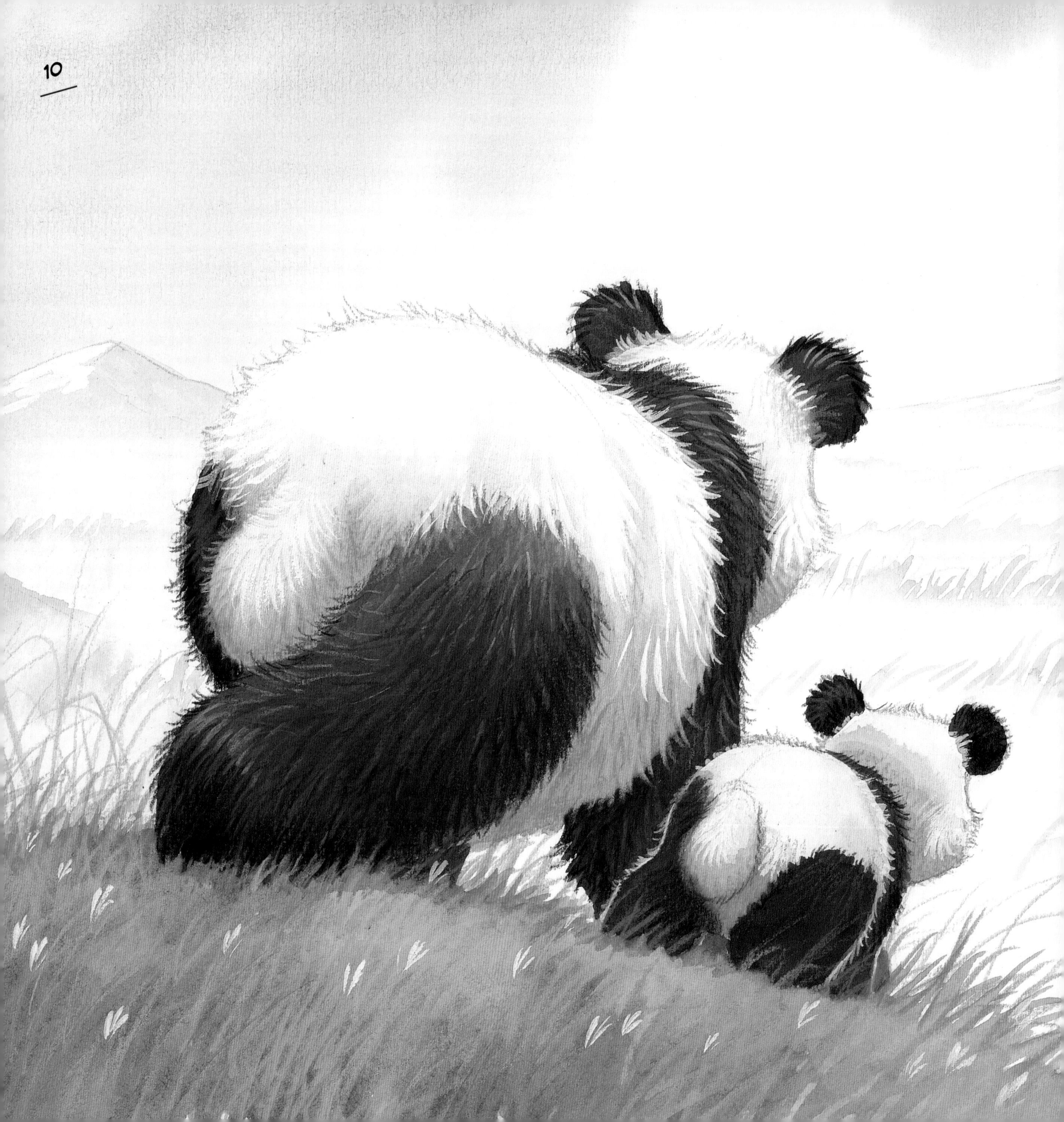

Rain had fallen while they were sleeping, and as the warm sun
gently heated the valley, a soft mist filled the air.
The valley was full of bamboo. Mommy knew the best shoots
to pick and she soon found a good spot.

"Come here, my baby," she cooed. "Snuggle in closely
and I will find us some yummy shoots."
As Little Panda munched the shoots, she wondered if
she could ever be happier than this.

The end of the day was always Little Panda's favorite.
As she stared at the bright moon peeping out from the bamboo,
she felt safe and warm and protected.

Their days were filled with lots
of walking and plenty of munching.
It takes a lot of bamboo to fill
a panda's tummy.

Life had not always been like this for pandas.
Her mom had told her stories of when men
had cut down huge forests of bamboo and
the pandas' tummies had ached with hunger.

She had told tales of how hunters used to stalk the forest.
But everything was safe now. No danger lurked
here anymore, just fun.

So Little Panda
learned to climb.

And she learned that
sometimes you fall.

With a lovely, soft mommy to cuddle,
even the difficult things could be fun.

She grew big and strong.
She grew up knowing
everything about how
to survive in this beautiful,
wild valley.

The day came when her mommy told her that she was fully grown. It was time to go out into the world on her own. They hugged for a long time. "I will love you forever," they whispered to each other.

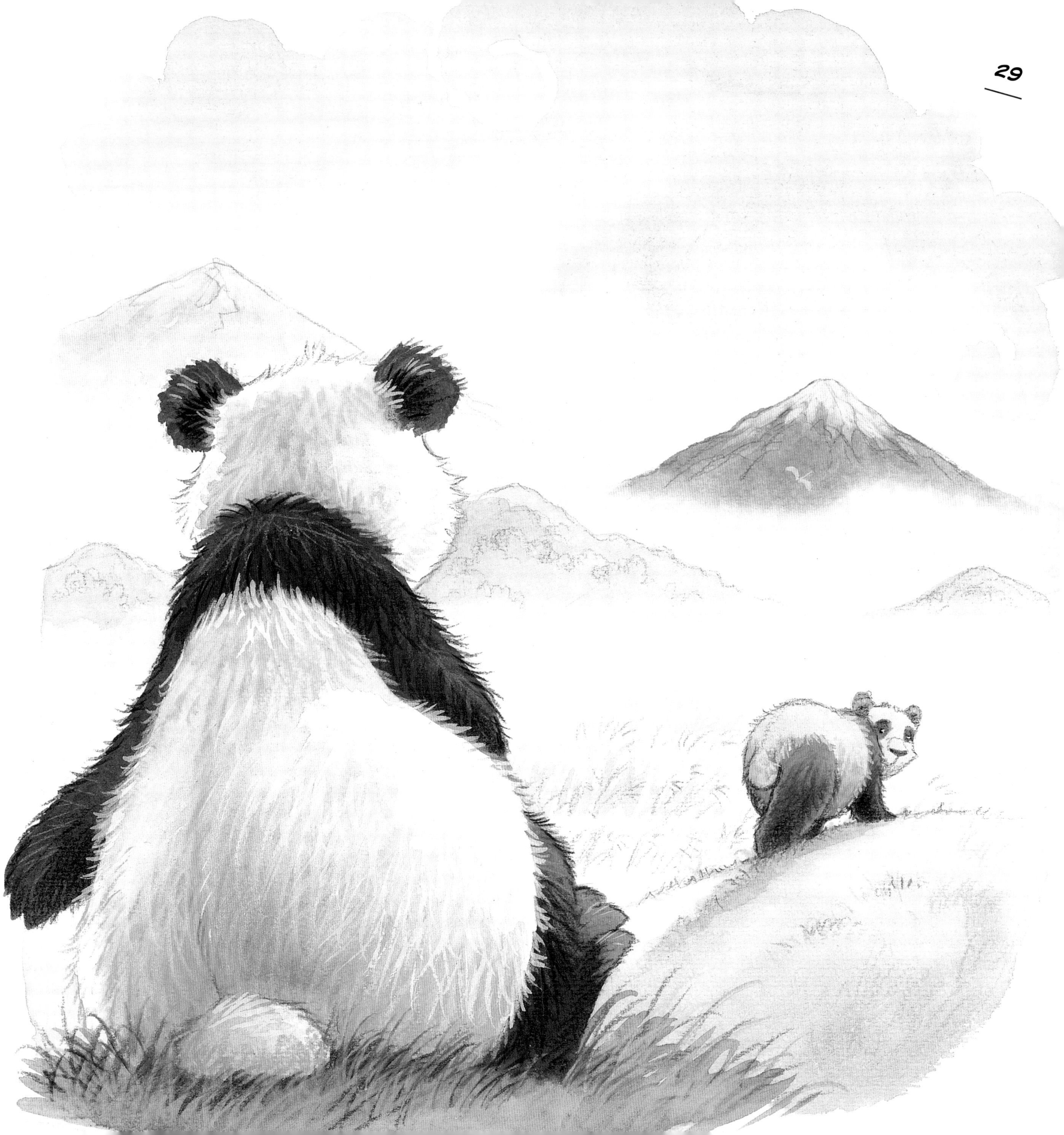

Now here Panda sits. She is grown up. And cradled in her giant paws, she has something that has made her even happier than she could ever dream.

Her own Little Panda. She will tell him all the wisdom
of the forest; she will love him, cuddle him, and protect him.
He is their future and all her love will raise him.

What **makes** me feel **happy**

This story is about a time of plenty.
The panda is now a
"protected species."
Do the children know what
this term means?

A protected species is a term
for animals that have been under
threat or endangered.

Many animals are still very limited in numbers.
It could be that their forest is being cut down,
like the orangutan's. It could be that global warming is
melting their icy home, like the polar bear's.
So what changed for the panda?

The Chinese people realized
that the panda was very unique.
It is a symbol.

They are now breeding pandas in captivity to increase
their numbers. They hope to release them into the wild.
They protect their habitat.
They encourage many people from other countries
to visit China just to see the panda.
They are now a very valued species.

So how many endangered species do the children think
there may be in our world?
Can they name any other animals that
they know are endangered?

There are currently about
5,000 endangered animal species
on our planet.

Many more than that have become extinct.
Do the children understand this word?
They are animals that once walked, or flew,
or swam on our planet. Some died after natural disasters,
such as the dinosaurs.
Others were hunted to extinction by humans,
such as the dodo.

Take a look at these animals
with the children.

What Makes Me Happy?

Sky Pony Press books may be purchased in bulk at special discounts for sales promotion, corporate gifts, fund-raising, or educational purposes. Special editions can also be created to specifications. For details, contact the Special Sales Department, Racehorse for Young Readers, 307 West 36th Street, 11th Floor, New York, NY 10018 or info@skyhorsepublishing.com.

Sky Pony® is a registered trademark of Skyhorse Publishing, Inc.®, a Delaware corporation.

Visit our website at www.skyhorsepublishing.com.

10 9 8 7 6 5 4 3 2 1

Author: Heidi Howarth
Illustrations: Daniel Howarth
Design and layout: Gemser Publications, S.L.
Cover design: Mona Lin

Library of Congress Cataloging-in-Publication Data is available on file.

Print ISBN: 978-1-5107-4551-3
Ebook ISBN: 978-1-5107-4565-0

Printed in China